WE HAVE WITH US

YOUR
SKY

WE HAVE WITH US

YOUR

SKY

MELANIE
HUBBARD

SUBITO PRESS 2012

ISBN: 978-0-9831150-4-5

Design & typesetting by HR Hegnauer | www.hrhegnauer.com
Text typeset in Joanna.

Subito Press
Department of English
University of Colorado at Boulder
226 UCB
Boulder, CO 80309-0226
subitopress.org

Distributed by Small Press Distribution
1341 Seventh Street
Berkeley, California 94710
spdbooks.org

Generous funding for this publication has been provided by
the Creative Writing Program in the Department of English and
the Innovative Seed Grant Program at the University of Colorado
at Boulder.

subito

for Mac

I

II

III

I

I have been trying to learn to read this summer, but I think it is a forlorn case. I read too fast and seem to have something in my mouth. The difficulty seems to be partly in the voice. The reading hour is a sad time for those of us who are afraid of our voices. Julia says that sometimes when it comes to her it seems as though it was impossible to speak a loud word. We have to read so very loud, even to the very top of the scale sometimes.

—LUCY THURSTON GOODALE
Mount Holyoke Female Seminary, Letter, August 8, 1838

Now suppose there had been phonographs in the Garden of Eden, and there had been handed down to us the cylinders recording the conversation that took place from the morning of man's birth until he was driven from out the gates of Paradise.

—"The Good the Speech Recorder Might Have Done."
Electrical Review, August 25, 1888

THE SUPPLE HELLION

Because I haven't a pinnacle hat
and here abandon trips, I pray

a hedge around me, hum
and stare on the harrow benches
with the hopers and the lifers.

Past the savage abbeys
the hiss-master slips the vise
and stuns a hoper by the river
playing her woolen vibes.

Now who's a brittle widow?
Willow, I mean
and the shadows long.

Punk, like cork, walks
the water & stops the wine.

I wheel a little higher
over the mirrored lanes.
I keep my appointments.

AT ONCE

I send my snaky regrets.
The gramophone was waiting

by the gates. At loose
ends, I gave it a crank & out

flew Tennyson's voice,
a cylinder coiled with grief.

The tilt turned revolutions
back a million years, the garden

curled to waste. Enemy
encampments in the fields

wunk out at dawn and left
a nest of roasted eggs.

They won't explode.
They're probably good.

WATER JOURNAL

The drain in the floor means 'stall,'
so you're not here

under your own power—
you've been scarfed, they call it,

flipped through the mirror like a dime
winks into a puddle.

Gather, like a curtain, your mouth
and eyes, your thin black hair,

the way you rhyme through a hole.
Gravitation has been such a drag,

but the corridor is clear
and bright tonight, and the assembly

went well. Some of your atoms
are missing, others derive from the ambient

litter in space. Here's your face:
your eye's enhanced, can't you see

a distant forefinger
stirring the first waves of creation.

A FIVE-STAR HOTEL

When I was a boy, the blast occurred.
Scurvy is in. So we arrange rides
for the oranges in our care.

We disembark, quenched. Do you remember
the yellow jalopy, Penelope?
She coughed and we knew it.

Listen, brother, you've gone glaiket—
gape-mouthed, stunned, or simply off, perhaps
to walls of blood. Will you be staying?

Skip the soda water. Soi-disant letters
are cold witnesses. So what shoes
fit the dead? Sunrise:

I hack and hack the spangled grasses.
Disco dew. Katherine Hepburn dew.
Nobody knew me. I knew no one.

ORIENTATION

You may pick up your hair shirt at check-in.
Laundry will be collected once a year.
May we suggest you save your nail clippings,

as they make a fine ash for our soap.
What is 'normal' is a common
question here. Deviate at your peril.

It is possible to spend the day untangling
strands, and we encourage this. Meditation, obsession.
Obsession, compulsion. Compulsion, perfection.

These are the ladders to Heaven.
To be free is an equation.
At this rate, they'll be done in 200 years.

They take an awful lot of cigarette breaks.
We keep them in the basement where it's relatively cool.
We have everything in canisters labeled

by predominant element. Molybdeum is my favorite.
Atrium is not an element. Neither is vacuum.
A vacuum is a tamed black hole. We have three.
	Don't open them.

You can get materials, but not help.

Help will be deducted from your debit account,

which is empty. We suggest you begin with the black keys.

HARM GARDEN

in the harm garden, reading

twenty neighbors and a cold electric bell

sleepy aspect of fog

skates on the hat tree

our host has gone abroad in a tight suit

pocket the tooth

feel it near your skin

TAKE ME ALONG

The film devolves in brown.
It starts the instant you sit down.

At first the rhymes intend,
then breed. They find you

out in the next scene
covered with small hairs.

She's a bleeder, get the 'scope!
The doctor's trying to cope but

he's a doctor of literature pulled
from his chair by the maitre d'.

Help or we'll bounce you, so he helps.

WHAT TO GIVE

Paper endearments?
A thousand drifting spiderlings?

Little headache, less is more.
The divine harbor is closed, so

the limbic drones a homily on night
and the bones stray home.

You would be a man
tied up in cords of light, a stone

bowl of song. When you go
to the river do you dip regret?

A dog swims by, looking right, looking left,
bobbing with each paw press through the waves.

CODEX

Through heavy doors, the dust and silence,
a chained book cannot be read,
each side wall pierced—

St. Jerome in his study
compelled to climb over his books
probably from the beginning.

The truth is protected by wire-work
in summertime, when honey-questing bees
painted on each ceiling panel

rise high, and give place for the desks.
We have windows near Stygian darkness,
a cemetery of books. For as in the writers

of annals, your men have made my library gay.
As it began to snow, this skyline effect,
too slender to bear a title.

A DAY FOR DIFFICULT

A day for difficult pistachios: it rained.

       The sunfish head stood
on the plate. I pressed my nose against the screen, dislodging

some dust-alphabet pronounced by those who
sneeze, and stared at the kumquat tree in frequent

bloom.
       You're busy clasping and unclasping tongue
and teeth, bearing down on the suspected cavity to see

might it be a little soft? She turns to say
in sign, the precipice is not quite done.

MARY SHELLEY SPEAKS

'How I, then a young girl, came to think
of, and to dilate upon, so very hideous an idea?'

I can scarcely accuse myself of a personal intrusion
which was the formation of castles in the air—

but I was not confined to my own identity.
Anxious that I should prove myself worthy

but it proved a wet, ungenial summer.
There was the History of the Inconstant Lover

annoyed by the platitude of prose.
We are continually reminded of the story of Columbus
    and his egg:

He would rush away from his odious handiwork—
the dark *parquet*, the closed shutters, with the moonlight

struggling. *It was on a dreary night of November*
I bid my hideous progeny go forth

leaving the core and substance of it untouched.

CHAOS

Suddenly he realized
small errors proved catastrophic
he analyzed a monument's shadow
how nonlinear nature is
a picture of reality
charted on the older man's blackboard
pioneer-by-necessity
clouds are not spheres
wondering about coastlines
one wintry afternoon
there was a long hiatus
this assumption
the oscillatory, the skewed varicose
he went to visit Lorenz
don't form a selfish concept
a sausage in a sausage
is the solar system
I, too, was convinced
you can focus
the mystery of the universe
the ceaseless motion
with light poise
to Metropolis, Stein, & Stein
the flecked river
builds its own banks

an imaginary pinball machine
perhaps we should believe
if the image is complicated
there is no randomness
randomness is a red
Norman Packard was reading
in December 1977
when Lorenz walked into the room
you don't see something
it's a simple example
Lanford listened politely
Huberman looked out
in the back of their minds
odd-shaped traveling waves

ENTROPY

more fragile than types, thinner, and wore
  down quickly enough
    delicate tendrils

    for unless the author will take the responsibility
   of the pointing entirely on himself,

the tail of a comma,
  once broken free, might lodge
    between letters to punctuate lightly, very simply,
  or even haphazardly their manuscripts

    liberated as speedily as convenient

      and all your letters fall to pye

    the necessity of his *remaining in town, and
   in the printing office* ALL NIGHT.

with his awl-like bodkin

tho' she touchingly reopened the subject

the matter is clouded
    by overlapping references
        stubbornness and presumption

the usual pattern: his friends heard him read
    but molding plaster often stuck to the types
        and orphaned spacers produced monks,

                    blackened welts

        from their weight and brittleness, from
    blows, from picks and batters, which will happen
notwithstanding the greatest care, from fractures
    at the edges

        of the establishment loaded with many
        tons of type kept in this undisturbed state

these fragments often print as distinct, migrating flecks
such as writing 'Cortez' when you mean 'Balboa'

IN BINDINGS

would, whenever   the itself into several strata, separated by no marked
and vex him with   lines, but shading off imperceptibly from top to bottom, no-
re of his mind, and thing disturbing the order of their repose. There were, then,
                              composed of the great landholders who had

                    *

        red an
        river,
        ting,
        red a
        Eleven
        for bu
        red and
        ment f
        assess

lighted
RED AND
between
to be
ween T
To be
lamps
eween. Th
ordinary
een Th
ordina

*

Mount
Lord, in a flame of fire   Mat.22

brought us out

A GRAVE BLESSING

The sound of one hand cleaning

    The long shots and bell-shaped pines

        For even the smallest patience

    A half-opened umbrella

A stick of tone

AMPLE RHAPSODY

to inform the vehicle
of its own abandonment

to call readers to action
smaller investigations and searches that go on in the body

to argue
the vehicle of its own abandonment

to theorize smaller investigations and searches
that go on in the body

to evaluate the vehicle of its own
abandonment

to propose
smaller investigations and searches that go on in the body

to provoke thought
the vehicle of its own abandonment

to express feeling smaller
investigations and searches that go on in the body

to entertain the vehicle
of its own abandonment

to give aesthetic pleasure
smaller investigations and searches that go on in the body

CATCHWORDS

surrendered to a maternal aunt
reading over her shoulder

a stranger
almost always blurred

after curfew
attacking the abyss

instead of
the rage

    *

deep within a shell
the wager will be lost

all texts are undecidable
the position Heraclitus abandoned

henceforth democracy
music at night

what was needed
was resistance

    *

later it will turn out
there is an impact

words, she thought
vast metaphysical plot

the bleakest of crimes
in the way of lucid analysis

11

A studious blind man, who had mightily beat his head about visible objects, and made use of the explication of his books and friends to understand those names of light and colors which often came in his way, bragged one day, that he now understood what scarlet signified. Upon which his friends demanding, what scarlet was? The blind man answered, it was like the sound of a trumpet.

—JOHN LOCKE
Essay on Human Understanding, 1689

AWAKENED BY A FAR-OFF DISTRESS

Dishes, radios, whorls of bone
(as on a gramophone or wax cylinder)
your ears resemble

a windowpane held
in a wooden frame acts
as a diaphragm, an amplifier, as does water

(scratched with vibrations)
You don't know where she is, by the highway
furniture store dumpsters a crash,

or across the water | the ossicles
and adjacent bone. a guttural. a shriek.
(exquisitely formed)

It's 2 a.m. You open the window, you make up
the visuals yourself
like those vaulted rooms

in mansions of state or cathedrals—
the plaster dome, the whispering room.
To be one on whom nothing is lost

you have always wanted to hear
when you are old
the smallest sounds

responsible, even when blurred
by the electrical distortions of the telephone
yet behind those unprepossessing

flaps of skin and cartilage
structures of such delicacy:
the eardrum, pressure-sensitive,

the spiral-shaped cochlea
and the semi-circular canals,
the organs of our sense of balance.

That afternoon you'd called to report
the loose cow: "There's a calf near the highway;
looks like the fence is down."

"What color is it?" "Tawny."
"Like red?" "No, it's more gingery."
"A 'gingery cow,' is that what they call it?"

Your husband's whistling breath
sounds like a scream. You close the window.
Everything carries | everything else.

THE CATCH

I bite the inside of my breath

Pressed to the floor

Back of the throat

Red sleeping bag

Folded under my teeth

Under the new girl

Gathered with little pleats

Where is my red sleeping bag

WISTFUL APPROACH
TO THE OBSTACLE

dappling the scales.

chained to a lake of fire, which singeth.

to a thin-skinned redemption.

who put their trust in You.

I wake in a dream and stay there.

with the bands and pretty uniforms.

this is my optimum routine.

pretty lippy with the interloping roosters.

I get it exactly backwards.

and in the shade, the anomaly.

PUNCTIFORM HUT

My life is a triumph, a spring
detonation

I string with implacable
string.

Filament. Twine. Silks the
bejesus

round a world with a circling
moon.

Watch the tiny flashes, a kind of hat
energy.

When I smile a small amount of matter
will vanish.

DOWN DOG, SWALE FUCKER,

Complete this sentence
using fox, split or spilt.

Sometimes I can forgive. Some-
times. There's a hinge

on your temple;
let me smack it off.

Blood's left, a curtsy.
See me.

THE HARDASS APPROACH

Throw out the papaya guts,
head injuries
ripening in a plastic bag.

The unveiling of the president
forms a blurry pattern,
a weighted voice:

so bring your shovels.
If you spend your career doing X,
you build a stadium

of your child's soft skin.
For the ultimate good
your grade will be based on effort

and self-policing:
In one half of the garden
shrubs trim themselves.

A WISDOM TOOTH

I like these little parapets.
They tear up the furniture, make nests in our hair,
     crap everywhere, bite to be playful.

They fought the enclosures.
They were sturdy beggars, brigands, and whores.

Some of these are tweezers, some of these are twine.
The raucous and how it sounds to say it.

Ceremonious retreat, waxing
with the requirements of form.

A large black 4 on a bright yellow square.
Yogis disprove the essential nature of 'chair.'

The dust makes a fine table.
Music in the discordant air.

ANOTHER GOOD SIGN

One day your boss
will write an opera. Meanwhile,

les trés riches heures file by—
they give each other

head in the break room, tousle
the fine, sandy-colored hay

they never comb. Welcome home.
At least they're having fun

in the end zone. The victorious
hours butt heads, their backs against

the louvered closet doors, which cant
off their hinges.

THE LAST AVANT-GARDE

Youth wants
for a long time
secretly
that was the year

we were all
vast paper
murals
static

and classical
designates a place
where everybody is
wiggin in

I grew up
exemplary
an abyss
misjudged

THE VILLAGE IDIOM

Wants to take the tadpoles HOME, Dad.

    Quills a few inches at night, then reverts.

Would call the police if it would help.

    Lipreads the mouths of cannons after rain.

Implodes on the count of three.

THE ROAD TO EMMAUS

A man is never far from his doubts.
Shhh—I'm attempting to write my armoires.
And then a third man appeared in their midst

and walked with them. Later they agreed
they could tell, by the way he held their noses
and broke them in the little room

that he had been Jesus. "Jesus,
what a kook!" They both laughed,
holding their aching noses.

LAKE GALILEE

They're sailing little wooden boats
along the shore. Look! The master did

a back flip from the bow. If you saw
a monkey go over a cliff,

would you follow? Well, you would—
but I mean, a normal person—if you

were a normal person and not
the stinky monkey you have

become, wouldn't you turn
and sit in the dust

and begin to draw a circle
for that marble game

called 'circle,' and wouldn't you
be planning to win my best

red shooter, dragging your finger
around in the silken dirt?

DEFEAT OF THE SOLO VIBRANTIST

Some new company of strangers dials
my remote location, the titty-twisting tribe
I stalk with a perfectly rational cup.

Up in Gallery Two I attend
a concert for uncommon instruments
walled off from stage

and sound, amid a bickering
disgruntled bunch. One man opines my feet
aren't fuckable, a moll disdains

my queries re: her boots—
and the guy in golden epaulettes
comes up the stairs with a pair of French

diplomats. He leans kindly into my face:
I'm wanted at State, he whispers, I know
what they want me to know.

"SOME WOMB."

The dirigible drips
its skin in flames
and I must trim

the murder by half.
"The enormity
of your growing up"
—now? then?—I ask

the nice old lady to watch
my bag/me strip
                    in the airport

I lay irregular
eggs, curdled black and slick.
A letter-bomb begins

and ends with 'A,' Ben's
best Jonson curled in a tomb.

SANS FRACAS IN
THE HEDGE O' SILENCE

So the light stays bolted to the floor.
My pants stay on & your pants stay on.
We abide in tranquility. Beards

retain their birds & carnage nests.
And no one's killed
on the Green Bridge. The glass

ripples at the usual rate. The spiders
twine their suppers in a steady thread.
They ascend and descend

like angels. The train crosses the dark blue
river into a light blue sky: orange car, orange car,
white car, white car, white car.

LAUGHING AT THE CEILING

Some princesses sing like the birds.
But can be interrupted. They go, Hummmm.
You removed the foundation so

there could be no horizon, only interiors
jumbled like a continent. It was
a breeze. A hard joy. Chirp. I have lost

the crown and feathers of my holy
office. Let the red cord swing
from its ground.

III

A description of John Tawell, who murdered his mistress in Slough in 1844, was wired ahead of him as, disguised as a Quaker, he fled by rail to London, where the authorities soon spotted him. The device of his undoing was immediately and popularly labeled 'the cords that hung John Tawell.' The telegraph code at the time did not include the letter Q.

— CAROLYN MARVIN
When Old Technologies Were New

DRESSED LIKE A KWAKER

You were five: a lie.
You were ten. Have you ever lost

a friend, slowly or suddenly?
You strive to spin a quarter

on its edge: fillet of light: a face
and a house inside each other.

Mobled Queen, Mundo Lindo.
What a fabulous air you have about you.

Bullets ricochet to the north. Divine
a neater way, blast off in those glass

galoshes peeling mud.
Suck the spit from your teeth

toward your tongue. In the dark,
we'll identify you by that sound.

You cannot fail, you can only vary
from yourself like a coelacanth.

We have you in the nets.

WEDDINGS, GIFTS

You received gifts—
the girl and the dead man—

some food we could not eat
causes the birds to be abundant.

Your emotions never seem in proportion;
if money goes, let us borrow

tasteless water
riveted together.

At each important phase
women untie the dead;

a virgin is detached—
know then, that God is bound to act.

Ten perfections,
linen:

a young man,
labor pains.

Food offered by the dead:
both father and mother, married.

THE PEQUOTS

The Pequots were an item in the '60s.
They've since devolved like angels to the earth:
flecks of paper, cut from a book.

But now I'm off to the mills!
The sky's a mackerel page—
a clotted scum, no scrum. Scrim.

I try to explain the persistence of spirit, life-
force, urge. She smirks into an ear, then licks.
God's dead, I said, she says.

A LOOSE MOUNTAIN

Asteroid, "like a star" in
Language I don't understand, or the mouths
Of cannons after rain, they find you out
In the next scene:

Solve for X. My dress is cracked on
Elliptical paths, exposed and holding.
Moon, you won't be denied, you cry
O as you slip inside,

Undone. Unfurl the bud in the socket, the iron
Nut swollen with rust,
The key laid out as a wheel.

A flick of your wrist and
I'm alive. Goodnight.
Now I know your name.

SILK ROAD

How the moon walks
and how kindness replies,
full as morning's

three-part chord:
the prince, asleep
before the tired fireplace

in which dwindles a grey
flower, cuneiform—it stings
an instant like sweet black

tea or a doctor missing
teeth. In his dream the desert
thought blows home again.

ASLEEP ALL AFTERNOON

From graves or an etched glass
regret, what were you like when you were ten?

A deluded, wounded omnipotence,
the vexed question you

resist, like a tracing
in wax in steel in copper in water

scanning down an eclipse to the subject:

The circumstances of one's breath
pinned to the brain's chemise—

bone
mostly, who wants a friend. And skin—

Did that hair fall into your eyes, did they wait for you?
Slow you to a stop?

and the sheen of skin. We are possibly angels. Call again.
Call again.

SAIL FORTH

Oh you, a handle!
beneath the discordant wave
I am

    *

as a hammer | many explanations

    *

whole and blood
highly wrought

the light is perceived

the vogue been explored
by its own unassisted effulgence

    *

Then the problem is
their obsessive popular joke:
they pictured an iron hand,
the absolute United States.

This being the head
wee cannot the Dragon
See, ther's his comming
Wee are upon us

            *

and now mans salvation
when she by the stars

in the best illustration coalesce
divers kyndes of fishes

that Radiance

If we fix our attention
To the surface | crusted distinctions

Enter into new combinations whereat
It may again be thrown forth

            *

this equivocation
is deeply colored 'automatism'

to take at odds
the radiance | but he

he wishes to avoid
a stone

the term to be assimilated
the 'it' of rendering

a sort of reverence for events

    *

it is this and ethics
a novel universe | swelling into existence

while he held

by curious removes
for the star and to the taint of sadness

    *

in this chapter
fluid sea

*

his habits nervous restlessness
meditating
he produces, not knowing why

seething principles
shapes ever other shapes

*

staring down spectral images
I happened to place it on my breast

as of burning heat
strange sympathy and body

a knot | a drama

its broken law
could not be discovered

*

the divine divine sea
opens without meaning
the meaning through it

*

as of burning heat

*

a vast each other
and all our skin

one morning Milky Way
rag my mind

the moment, when waking thoughts start up

attempts, and the world
to speak the air

personify its prospects
it was | was mine

A HILL IN THE DISTANCE

The phone call from the lover
are broken. (Returned,

the intrusion shrugged.)
For he was only kidding

himself, deluded, so dearly
ashamed. For the promise within

are broken. Perhaps I would see
no one and have rather Sabbath feelings.

Perhaps to forgive, unceasingly singing.
To wander fireside, fretful

about nobody or someone are broken.
What's left is a language, a faithful

country, and one small, brown breast.
A shell, anguish are broken.

A SOLID WHITE BUTTRESS

Tubular buds you can eat, the frank
faces of lilies and cold stars

Amid towering ferns, the swollen coast
a fatigue sets in, but we have water

From a long way off, up the desert
something I respect in you

My handsome foe, my marvelous weather
a sudden sharp report

Like birds at a lake children scatter
in Nairobi, at the elephant hospital

THE JUDAS TREES

the judas trees blink
as they kiss | like lights

you are a disaster no one foretold
liebkind, wolf | hammer-like

the moon regrets its calls. sorry. sorry.
you respond to praise, static | antigone,

your brothers would avenge the hollow air

HAPPY NEW YEAR

They come spinning like the wheels of beasts
up to the auberge. They want breakfast

over the ashes of this house. Their breath
is rank and sore, their mottled voices

drift through the early dawn, their skin
is defiled and tastes like dirt, their hair is clotted.

They stand there limp with misdirection.
"Don't rain much on Tuesday," says one, by way

of introduction. The pallid colt of remorse
coasts into view. It's got a loopy gait.

The talking one steps up, so I hover three inches
off the floor, then zoom out the doorjamb

over their heads. Here comes the part
where I gun them down from behind after explaining

the no-smoking policy. My splayed revolver
wishes I'd go back on it. But I know they maundered

up to curse my children. *Noli me tangere*, I say
to no one now. I roll on, heavy and steaming.

GOD'S PLAN

The monks set up this house:
a series of concentric kitchens.

The outer, visitor-kitchen makes pies.
The inner, enlightened kitchen makes—airs—

visitors call it the 'courtyard' or even
the 'garden.' The intoning guide

does not correct them. Each morning
my chair has moved an inch. Our

history, our stricken beds. Under
my bed, dead wasps. Distress

is a garden. Who will jimmy
the lock—I, a pile of little stones

buried so long ago? Who will arrive
with the grease of compassion

and the four wheels of detachment?
If I could get this motor out of third,

if I could time my sighs with its jugular
chuffs, I could play myself a little song

and look back, a chasm of one,
on these sharp-nailed, useless terriers.

MY DUTY

Sir I am occupying my position.
The battlements still hold

but the dirt springs and the ton
shucks my buddy's arm, his wristwatch.

Why are there no women in me
to redden on his ragged

chest. Incoming, the spires and lights.
The lines are down on both ends,

a loosened tourniquet
in command, now, of nothing.

                *

Perspicacious of you, Sir: I am found
out along the perimeter, scoping the flags

of our foes. They hold fire, too easy
to kill a fool above ground, to cut

stick figures: better to watch the film
drifting over their eyes. Better to catch

dust in your mouths, watchers, and Sir!
I have misplaced my terrible ardor.

Choose which gun, Sir. Choose.

I SPY

The canting bitches what it hits
and whom we are walling in.

Position up here from the panopticon:
zip up, you're done. Jacket flapping

syntax is like garbles on a house, the ports
and pores of angels rib the gate. What

do you call that fray? An axed
six-burner baby in a brushed

steel hoodie. Kazaam! It was not
a cartoon, not funny. No one

in the corridor b'lieved. The office sneered
they b'lieved, their jumpsuits

shiny and black. Above are heroes,
they have telescopes:

they see the tiny vicious man
we are careful never to know—

There was an injun in here: I scale
the chiseled stone. Paisley. Domino.

A SCANDAL OVER THE CAUCASUS

The wind begins, passing
voices. Red cockaded woodpeckers drill
the bamboo, swing from cane to cane.

The mockingbird's sheer trill,
the bantam's pentameter chanticleer,
a dog's shriek above the waft of music.

Constant dog, oh shoot it. Smoke from the woodpile
thickens. Out of the garage a baby caws.
Whacking in the distance the flat roofing.

The highway washes like an ocean beyond dunes.
It's that the air is clear, and that the earth
is hollow. How does the water stay in?

A boat turns over water, little mill. The radio
soars beyond the cut of air. "Mom?"
a kid calls. Trees fall in.

GREEN INK IN A HEAVY HAND

Mom, the arctic fox's head came off.
Sigh. Go ahead, change your life—
see you next Tuesday. An old saw

& the blade sticks in the wood,
the screws jump out.
I can cobble this

house together, just gimme a sec.
And some glue. Something something
brains, something something fat.

She wants her cap, her bow
shrugged free of its gut. Swine
hustle along the fence. My sister

the beekeeper abhors them, my brother
the brewer the same. He herds those hops
in his jenny bed, he whinges

in his sleep, does Bro. The palings fray.
Think with me: we need an alibi
for those foxes burning through the corn.

ACKNOWLEDGMENTS

The author wishes to thank the editors of *Fence, Typo, Cannibal, Strange Machine, Forklift, OH, Swink, Cab/Net, Caketrain, Can We Have Our Ball Back, Shampoo, Cotelydon,* and *88: A Journal of Contemporary American Poetry,* where versions of some these poems first appeared. Thanks to Matt and Katy Henriksen for the beautiful work that went into publishing *Gilbi Winco Swags* (Cannibal Books, 2008), where versions of some of these poems first appeared. Thanks to the many authors whose works informed these poems, including Henry Petroski, Mary Shelley, James Gleick, David Lehman, Allan Dooley, Carolyn Marvin, and Lewis Hyde. "In Bindings" is made up of the tattered remains of book pages bound into the spines of three nineteenth-century friendship albums. Thanks to Mt. Holyoke College Archives & Special Collections for the Lucy Goodale quote. Thanks to the Hillsborough County Arts Council for a grant to support my time at the Juniper Summer Writing Institute; thanks to Dara Wier, Matthew Zapruder, and Matthea Harvey for helpful critique and encouragement there. Thanks to the Atlantic Center for the Arts for an incredibly generative experience and to Brenda Hillman for receptive attention to some of these poems. Thanks very much to Julie Carr for selecting this work, and to Noah Eli Gordon for squiring it through the publication process. Thank you to HR Hegnauer for amazing design work, and to Kylie Miller for permission to use the cover art. Special thanks to my poetry crew: Sharon Mitchell, Lisa White, and Harry Brody. Thanks to Mom, Dad, and Chris. And thanks beyond measure to my husband, Mac Miller, and my daughter, Kylie Miller, for everything.

ABOUT THE AUTHOR

Melanie Hubbard lives in a small town on the west coast of Florida with her family. She received a PhD in literature from Columbia University; she also received a National Endowment for the Humanities research fellowship to do a scholarly book, now being revised, on Emily Dickinson. She has taught at New College of Florida, Eckerd College, and the University of Tampa. Poems, reviews, scholarly articles, and personal essays have appeared in a variety of periodicals. A chapbook, *Gilbi Winco Swags*, was published by Cannibal Books in 2008.

ABOUT SUBITO PRESS

Subito Press is a non-profit literary publisher based in the Creative Writing Program of the Department of English at the University of Colorado at Boulder. Subito Press encourages and supports work that challenges already-accepted literary modes and devices.

SUBITO PRESS

Noah Eli Gordon, *director*
Stephen Daniel Lewis, *managing editor*
Shari Beck
Alissa Fehlbaum
Courtney Morgan
Nick Kimbro
Caroline Davidson
Sara Marshall
Michael Shirzadian
Tanner Hadfield
Catherine Willits

SUBTIO PRESS TITLES

2008

    Little Red Riding Hood Missed the Bus by Kristin Abraham

    With One's Own Eyes: Sherwood Anderson's Realities

        by Sherwood Anderson

        Edited and with an Introduction by Welford D. Taylor

    My Untimely Death by Adam Peterson

    Dear Professor, Do You Live in a Vacuum? by Nin Andrews

2009

    Self-Titled Debut by Andrew Farkas

    F-Stein by L.J. Moore

2010

    Song & Glass by Stan Mir

    Moon Is Cotton & She Laugh All Night by Tracy Debrincat

    Bartleby, the Sportscaster by Ted Pelton

2011

    The Body, The Rooms by Andy Frazee

    Death-in-a-Box by Alta Ifland

    Man Years by Sandra Doller

2012

    We Have With Us Your Sky by Melanie Hubbard

    Vs. Death Noises by Marcus Pactor